Our **WILD**™
WORLD
SERIES

Wolves

NORTHWORD
Minnetonka, Minnesota

DEDICATION
For my pack—Mom, Dad, and Kai—with love.

© NorthWord Press, 2000

Photography © 2000: Rita Groszmann: front cover, back cover, pp. 4, 14, 22-23, 36; Mark Raycroft: p. 5; Michael H. Francis: pp. 6-7, 20, 25, 29, 30-31, 33, 42, 43; Tom & Pat Leeson: pp. 8, 19, 26-27; Erwin & Peggy Bauer: pp. 10-11, 44; Robin Brandt: p. 13; Craig Brandt: pp. 16-17; Lisa & Mike Husar: pp. 34-35; Howie Garber/www.wanderlustimages.com: pp. 38-39, 40.

Illustrations by John F. McGee
Designed by Russell S. Kuepper
Edited by Barbara K. Harold

NorthWord Books for Young Readers
11571 K-Tel Drive
Minnetonka, MN 55343
1-888-255-9989
www.tnkidsbooks.com

Library of Congress Cataloging-in-Publication Data

Evert, Laura.
    Wolves / by Laura Evert ; illustrations by John F. McGee.
        p. cm. (Our wild world series)
    ISBN 1-55971-748-3 (soft cover)
    1. Wolves--Juvenile literature. [1. Wolves. 2. Endangered species.] I. McGee, John F.
  II. Title. III. Series.
    QL737.C22 E94 2000
    599.773--dc21   00-028383

Printed in Malaysia

Our WILD™ WORLD SERIES

Wolves

Laura Evert
Illustrations by John F. McGee

NORTHWORD
Minnetonka, Minnesota

DO YOU THINK dogs are related to wolves? They are! All dogs—from the smallest to the largest—are descendants of an ancient breed of wolf.

Today, wolves live in many different parts of the world. Besides the United States, wolves can also be found in Canada, Mexico, Russia, Europe, and China. There are two species (SPEE-sees), or kinds, of wolves living in North America today: gray wolves and red wolves.

When you picture a wolf in your mind, you are probably thinking of a gray wolf. Gray wolves are large with big, pointed ears and a bushy coat with long hair. But they are not always gray. They can be white, black, rusty red, tan, or even a combination of colors.

Wolves have a large brain, and scientists believe they are very intelligent.

Timber wolves of the same family may have coats of completely different colors.

Gray wolves are also known as timber wolves, tundra wolves, Arctic wolves and Mexican wolves, depending on where they live. Male gray wolves are about 6 feet (1.8 meters) long from nose to tail tip. The bushy tail itself may be 18 inches (45 centimeters) long. Adult male wolves weigh about 65 to 120 pounds (29.5 to 54 kilograms). They stand about 3 feet (91 centimeters) high at the shoulder. Females are smaller.

Most of the gray wolves in North America are called timber wolves. They can be found in many of the northern states. There are just over 9,200 wolves in the United States today. Alaska has the largest number of wolves: 7,000. Minnesota is next with 2,000 wolves. The rest live in other states including Montana, Michigan, Idaho, Washington, Wisconsin, and Wyoming. There are about 60,000 wolves throughout the provinces of Canada.

Wolves can leap great distances,
even over streams while they are running.

Wolves, like this red wolf, learn at a young age
to be alert to anything that may be prey or danger.

Red wolves are much smaller than gray wolves. In fact, with their pointed noses and smaller size, red wolves look more like coyotes. Their fur also has specks of red in it, which is how they got their name. From nose to tail tip, red wolves are about 4 feet (1.2 meters) long. They usually weigh about 60 pounds (27 kilograms).

Only a few small groups of red wolves can be found in some eastern states such as Tennessee and North Carolina.

Scientists who study animals are called zoologists (zoe-OL-uh-jists). They are closely observing timber wolves and red wolves to learn more about them.

Wolves
FUNFACT:

The scientific name for the gray wolf is *Canis lupus;* the red wolf is *Canis rufus.*

Pages 10-11: The different colors in a wolf's coat provide camouflage, or help it blend in with the surroundings.

Wolves have a rounder and wider head than their dog relatives. They have yellow-green eyes, and better eyesight than humans. Wolves have good vision, especially at night when they often hunt. They are able to detect motion from long distances.

The wolf's sense of hearing is far better than a human's. They can hear another wolf's howl from as far away as six miles!

But even a good sense of hearing is not the wolf's strongest sense. With a long, slender snout, the wolf has an excellent sense of smell. Wolves can smell other animals from over a mile away, which is at least a hundred times better than a person can smell.

A good sense of smell is very important to a wolf's survival, especially in winter. Wolves do not hibernate, or sleep through the winter, as some other animals do. They spend much of their time hunting, but only when necessary because it uses precious energy. They eat as much as possible when they can so they don't have to hunt again so soon. When wolves are not hunting, they rest to save their strength and conserve their energy.

When hunting, a wolf moves carefully and quietly, concentrating with all its senses.

Wide paws with thick fur help wolves walk across the snow
without sinking too far, like snowshoes do for people.

A wolf's coat of hair keeps it warm throughout the cold winter months. In the fall, wolves grow a soft, woolly fur called an undercoat next to their skin. The undercoat holds in the heat from their body and insulates them from the cold.

On top of the undercoat are long guard hairs. These completely cover the undercoat with waterproof protection against rain or snow. In the spring, the undercoat is shed to keep the wolf cool in the warmer weather.

Another way wolves keep themselves warm is to curl up into a tight ball and wrap their long, thick tail over their nose. To protect their feet, or paws, they tuck them underneath their body.

And wolves don't mind getting snowed on—if the snow completely covers their body it adds another layer of insulation against the wind and cold!

Wolves
FUNFACT:

A wolf's winter coat can be up to 3 inches (7.6 centimeters) thick. It keeps the wolf warm in temperatures as cold as -50° Fahrenheit (-45° Centigrade).

Pages 16-17: Like dogs, wolves pant to release extra body heat, which helps them stay cool on hot summer days.

A wolf's four legs are strong. They help the wolf travel long distances without becoming tired, even in snow. The front paws are about 4 inches (10 centimeters) wide and 5 inches (12.7 centimeters) long. The hind, or back, paws are smaller. Each paw has four toes and four sharp claws.

Wolves are carnivores (KAR-nuh-vorz), which means that they are meat-eating animals. For food, wolves mostly hunt animals with hooves such as deer, caribou, moose, elk, and wild sheep. These animals are called prey (PRAY), which means they are hunted for food by other animals. Since wolves are large animals, their prey must be even larger to provide enough food. Wolves usually hunt animals that are young, very old, or sick because they are easier to catch.

Adult wolves can eat as much as 20 pounds (9 kilograms) of meat at one meal! When they cannot find any large prey species, wolves eat rabbits, birds, and rodents, such as mice and voles. They also eat some plants and berries.

Wolves must drink plenty of water to keep up their energy and stay healthy.

Wolves are very social animals, which means they hunt and live in groups called packs. The members of the pack are usually related to one another. A pack is made up of five to ten wolves, but in areas where there is plenty of food, as many as twenty wolves can form a pack.

Each wolf pack has two leaders, one male and one female, called alphas. They are easy to identify in the group because they are the ones holding their head high with their ears forward. They decide where the pack lives, where they hunt, what they eat, and when they rest. Usually only the alpha wolves mate and have babies, called pups.

The alphas set the rules and make sure all the other wolves obey them.

Standing still and with its ears pointed forward, this alpha is trying to identify a sound.

Each wolf has its own place in the pack, with special responsibilities and duties. They all know what their place is according to a system called a hierarchy (HI-er-ark-ee).

Sometimes a wolf may challenge one of the alphas to try to become the new leader. They rarely fight, but they test each other's strength. Sometimes the alpha can stop the challenge with a long stare. Other times the alpha must growl and even nip at the other wolf until it backs down. When the other wolf knows it is defeated, it tucks its tail between its legs and looks at the ground. It may lie down and roll over on its back. Sometimes it may even slowly crawl over to the alpha, which is the signal for, "I've learned my lesson. I will obey!"

Returning pack members often sniff each other's nose to tell where they have been and if they found food.

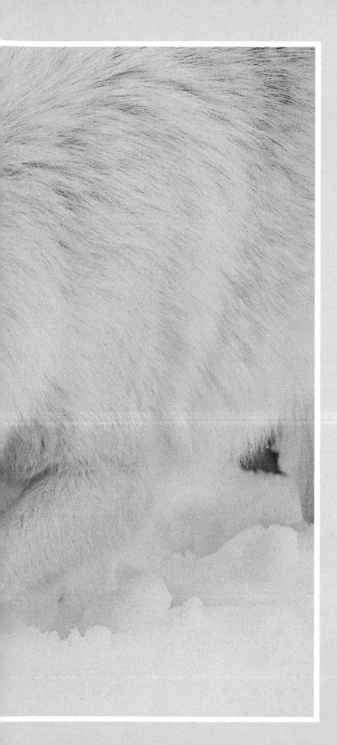

Next in line in the pack hierarchy is the beta (BAY-tuh) wolf. The beta is also considered to be a leader in the pack, but it is second in command to the alphas. The beta wolf helps the alphas with the discipline of the other wolves, especially when the alphas are not nearby. And when there are pups, it is the beta wolf that has the responsibility of babysitting while the parents hunt for food.

The lowest member of the wolf pack is called the omega (o-MAY-guh) wolf. The other wolves often chase and tease the omega. Sometimes they are mean to the omega, and it is usually the last wolf allowed to eat.

All of the wolves in between the beta and the omega are called biders (BI-derz). They have this name because they are neither the leaders nor the omega. They are simply "biding their time," waiting for their chance to become an alpha someday.

Pack members are very affectionate toward each other. They protect one another, snuggle together to keep warm, howl together, and help groom, or clean, each other. They also do most of their hunting together.

Wolves can go a very long time without eating. Sometimes bad weather prevents them from hunting, or they do not find enough prey. If there was plenty of meat in their last meal, wolves can wait to eat again for up to two weeks. And then they will eat as much as possible at one time.

When wolves eat, they consume, or ingest, bones and hair from their prey along with the meat. Although the bone pieces are sharp and jagged, they do not hurt the wolf. This is because the wolf's digestive system uses the hair to wrap around the bone pieces, allowing them to pass more easily through the wolf. Wolf droppings, called scat, are easy to identify. They look like hard, tube-shaped masses of hair.

Wolves
FUNFACT:

A wolf's sense of hearing is so good that it can hear a mouse moving underneath a thick layer of snow.

Wolves often eat with big bites and gulps,
which is how we got the phrase "hungry as a wolf."

Wolves may catch their prey in different ways. They can trot at a steady speed of about 5 miles (8 kilometers) per hour for many hours. This is usually long enough to tire most prey species, making them vulnerable to attack. Wolves are also fast runners when it comes time for the chase. They can run as fast as 35 miles (56 kilometers) per hour in short bursts.

Although some prey animals can run faster than wolves, wolves may still have the advantage because they hunt together. When they locate their prey, the wolves separate and travel in different directions until they form a wide circle around the prey. Now the prey has nowhere to run and the wolves can move closer without having to run as fast.

Wolves do not usually follow their prey into the water of a lake or river. This means that some prey animals are able to escape. Wolves may, however, catch prey that they have chased onto the ice of a frozen lake or river in the winter.

Pack members hunting together are much more successful than a wolf hunting on its own.

A pack lives and hunts in an area called its home territory. A home territory is at least 50 square miles (130 square kilometers) in size. Some can be as large as 100 square miles (260 square kilometers). Wolves protect their home territory and force out other wolves that try to trespass. There is usually an area between the territories of two packs called the buffer zone. It keeps the packs safely apart, and helps avoid fights and competition for food.

A habitat is the kind of place where animals (or people) can live. A good habitat for wolves provides plenty of food, water, and a place to raise their young. Wolves usually prefer to live in large wooded areas far away from people.

The amount of food in a habitat determines the size of a pack's territory, and the number of wolves in a pack. When there is plenty of food, a pack can have a smaller territory and more members. Sometimes, if the pack becomes very large, it may split into two packs.

But if food is scarce, some wolves are forced out of the pack to be on their own. These wolves are called loners (LO-nerz). Loners may try to join another pack because it is much easier to hunt in a group than by themselves. But other packs usually do not let loners join them, especially if food is hard to find. Sometimes several loners will form their own pack. And sometimes a male and female loner will mate, have pups, and start a pack of their own.

Wolves
FUNFACT:

In the wild, wolves live
as long as 10 years.

Wolves sometimes need good balance, like this wolf crossing a river by jumping from rock to rock.

The best place for wolves to live, hunt, and raise their pups is in a large
territory. Unfortunately, this kind of habitat is becoming scarce.

The alpha male and female usually mate and stay together for their whole lives. They mate in late winter or early spring. After mating, the alpha female looks for a place to have her pups. This place is called a den, and can be a cave or a large, hollow log. If the female cannot find a den that she likes, she might make her own. Sometimes she uses the burrow of another animal. Sometimes she digs her own den in the ground.

The den is usually located on a high point in the pack's home territory. It must be warm and dry, but close to water so the mother can drink without being away from her pups for very long. The other females in the pack help her make the den ready for the pups. Sometimes wolves use the same den year after year.

About nine weeks after mating, the female gives birth to her pups in the den while her mate stands guard outside. Wolves may have as many as ten pups at a time, but four to six is the usual number. When the pups are born they weigh about 1 pound (453 grams) and they cannot see or hear. They press against their mother for warmth. They nurse from her, drinking the milk that they need to grow strong.

Pups spend the first two weeks just sleeping and eating, then they are able to open their eyes for the first time. After three weeks, they can hear and they begin to move around the den, always staying close to their mother.

During this time, the other members of the pack bring the mother food to eat so she does not have to leave the pups. They bring the food to the entrance of the den and leave it there. They do not disturb her or the pups.

Curious young pups are not allowed to stray too far from their safe and warm den.

When pups are hungry they lick the mouth
of the adults to let them know it's time to be fed.

When the pups are about four weeks old, they are ready to go out of the den. The pack members howl with excitement when they meet the new pups for the first time. They all take turns licking and nuzzling the pups so they get to know each other. They also protect the pups from predators, or enemies, such as hawks and eagles. Each night the pups and mother go back into the den to sleep where it is safe and warm.

Even young pups howl to get attention, and to show that they are members of the pack.

When the pups are nine weeks old, their mother takes them to join the pack. They leave the den for good. It is time for the mother to hunt again with the other wolves. While the pack is away hunting, at least one wolf stays behind to take care of the pups in an area called the rendezvous (RON-day-voo) site. It is a safe place for the pups. Like the den, a wolf pack may use the same rendezvous site for many years.

Summer is a fun time for the pups. They chase each other and tease the babysitter by pulling on his tail and ears. They also play-fight with one another, which helps make them strong. It also helps them learn their places in the hierarchy of the pack.

When the pups are still very young and not able to chew well, many of the adults help them eat. The adult chews and swallows the food first, so that it is partially digested and soft. When the pup is hungry the adult brings up the food from its stomach for the pup to eat. When a young pup is very hungry it will beg for food by licking and nipping at the mouths of the adults.

When the pups are a little older, the adults bring them small prey animals, such as mice and birds, to eat. Next they bring live prey so the pups can learn how to hunt for themselves. Finally, when the pups are about one year old, they begin to hunt with the pack for their own food.

Wolves
FUNFACT:

Pups from the same litter can have coats of different colors.

Some people think wolves spend much of their time howling at the moon. While it is true that wolves do howl in the moonlight, there are many other times that they howl, and for many different reasons.

A wolf may howl to warn other wolves that they are in its territory. Wolves also howl after a successful hunt. One wolf usually starts the howl and the rest of the pack joins in. Sometimes wolves seem to howl just for the fun of it. And they usually howl very loudly. They also jump around and act very excited. Zoologists don't know why they do this, but the wolves seem to enjoy it.

Howling helps strengthen the bonds of the pack. Wolves learn to identify each pack member by the sound of its howl. Pack members communicate by howling when they are out of sight of one another. When a wolf howls, at least one member of its pack is sure to answer.

The howl of a wolf can travel great distances, letting all who hear it
know that the territory has been claimed by a pack.

Wolves growl and show their teeth when challenged by other wolves and to keep lower pack members in their place.

Even at a young age the pups join in the howl with their puppy-like yips and high-pitched yowling. Some people say a wolf pack howl is like a beautiful song of the wilderness.

Wolves make sounds other than howls to communicate. These noises are called vocalizations (vo-cul-i-ZA-shunz). They bark, growl, whine, cry, and yip. Each of these sounds has a different meaning. Whimpering and whining among pack members, for example, is a sign of friendliness and affection. Wolves may make a barking sound when they are nervous, and they growl to chase away other wolves.

Wolves also communicate with their tails. Everyone knows that a dog wags its tail when it is happy. Wolves wag their tails too, for the same reason. They wag their tails when they see one another after time apart, or when their packmates return with food. They also wag their tails when the alpha wolf approaches them in a friendly way, and when the pups come out of the den for the first time.

When a wolf holds its tail straight out, it means that it is concentrating on something, like the smell of nearby prey.

Since each wolf has its own place in the pack, a wolf also uses its tail to let the others know its place in the hierarchy. For example, an alpha wolf often holds its tail high and the omega wolf may hold its tail between its legs.

Wolves
FUNFACT:

Wolves have 42 teeth. Some of them, called canine teeth, are over 1 inch (2.54 centimeters) long.

This wolf may be howling to let the pack know how far away it is and what direction it is traveling.

Wolves use scent, or odor, to communicate with each other, too. By leaving their scent around the edges of their territory, they let members of their pack and wolves from other packs know the boundaries. Wolf scat and urine contain scent. As a wolf travels in its territory, it leaves urine and scat to mark its territory.

Wolf tracks also contain the scent of the wolf. A wolf track has four oval-shaped toe marks and a large, upside-down heart shape where the paw pad touched the ground. At the end of the toe marks you can often see deep, round marks where the claws dug in for traction.

If the tracks are close together, the wolf was probably walking. The farther apart the tracks are, the faster the wolf was walking or running.

Wolf tracks usually appear in a straight line because wolves place one foot in front of the other as they walk.

These wolf pups are leaving the den for the first time,
eager to explore their new world.

Centuries ago, wolves roamed, or wandered, across much of North America in great numbers. There may have been as many as 2 million wolves at one time. But as more and more people moved across the country, wolves ran out of room to live and hunt. Some people are afraid of wolves, even though wolves prefer to stay as far away from people as possible. These things make life very difficult for wolf packs.

To help increase the number of wolf packs in North America, some wolves have been moved from places that have many wolves to places that have only a few wolves. For instance, Yellowstone National Park in Wyoming has received some new wolves. And zoologists continue to study them in their new habitat.

Wolves are fighting a battle to survive as more and more people move into their habitat. Wolves are listed as an "endangered species" everywhere in the United States except Alaska and Minnesota. Endangered means that the species is nearly extinct in its habitat. Many people are working hard to be sure there will always be wolves living and howling in the wild.

Wolves
FUNFACT:

The biggest wolf on record weighed over 225 pounds (101 kilograms).

Internet Sites

You can find out more interesting information about wolves and lots of other wildlife by visiting these Internet sites.

www.animal.discovery.com   Discovery Channel Online

www.fws.gov/   U.S. Fish and Wildlife Service

www.kidsplanet.org   Defenders of Wildlife

www.nationalgeographic.com/kids   National Geographic Society

www.nwf.org/kids   National Wildlife Federation

www.wolf.org   The International Wolf Center

www.wolfcenter.org   The Wolf Education and Research Center

www.worldwildlife.org   World Wildlife Fund

http://nature.org/   The Nature Conservancy

Index

Titles available in the Our Wild World Series:

ALLIGATORS AND CROCODILES
ISBN 978-1-55971-859-2

BATS
ISBN 978-1-55971-969-8

BISON
ISBN 978-1-55971-775-5

BLACK BEARS
ISBN 978-1-55971-742-7

BUTTERFLIES
ISBN 978-1-55971-967-4

CARIBOU
ISBN 978-1-55971-812-7

CHIMPANZEES
ISBN 978-1-55971-845-5

COUGARS
ISBN 978-1-55971-788-5

COYOTES
ISBN 978-1-55971-983-4

DOLPHINS
ISBN 978-1-55971-776-2

EAGLES
ISBN 978-1-55971-777-9

FALCONS
ISBN 978-1-55971-912-4

GORILLAS
ISBN 978-1-55971-843-1

HAWKS
ISBN 978-1-55971-886-8

LEOPARDS
ISBN 978-1-55971-796-0

LIONS
ISBN 978-1-55971-787-8

LIZARDS
ISBN 978-1-55971-857-8

MANATEES
ISBN 978-1-55971-778-6

MONKEYS
ISBN 978-1-55971-849-3

MOOSE
ISBN 978-1-55971-744-1

ORANGUTANS
ISBN 978-1-55971-847-9

OWLS
ISBN 978-1-55971-915-5

PENGUINS
ISBN 978-1-55971-810-3

POLAR BEARS
ISBN 978-1-55971-828-8

PRAIRIE DOGS
ISBN 978-1-55971-884-4

SEA TURTLES
ISBN 978-1-55971-746-5

SEALS
ISBN 978-1-55971-826-4

SHARKS
ISBN 978-1-55971-779-3

SNAKES
ISBN 978-1-55971-855-4

TIGERS
ISBN 978-1-55971-797-7

TURTLES
ISBN 978-1-55971-861-5

VULTURES
ISBN 978-1-55971-918-6

WHALES
ISBN 978-1-55971-780-9

WHITETAIL DEER
ISBN 978-1-55971-743-4

WILD HORSES
ISBN 978-1-55971-882-0

WOLVES
ISBN 978-1-55971-748-9

NORTHWORD
Minnetonka, Minnesota